A TALE OF TWO CHILMARKS

ENGLAND TO NEW ENGLAND

A TALE OF TWO CHILMARKS

England to New England

IONA SINCLAIR

Illustrations by John C. Atkinson

First published in the United Kingdom in 1994
by Chilmark Books

This edition published in the United Kingdom in 2009
by The Hobnob Press, PO Box 1838, East Knoyle, Salisbury, SP3 6FA
www.hobnobpress.co.uk

British Library Cataloguing in Publication Data
A catalogue record for this book is available from the British Library

ISBN 978-1-906978-11-2

Typeset in Scala 12.5/16pt. Typesetting and origination by John Chandler
Printed by Lightning Source

for the people of the Chilmarks

Contents

Acknowledgements

The help given by the Dukes County Historical Society and the American Museum in Britain, Bath, is gratefully acknowledged. Most of all, my most grateful thanks to John Atkinson, the fun and skill of whose drawings add immeasurably to the text.

I.S.

Stonehenge

Roman Road

Old Sarum

Chilmark

Wilton

Salisbury

Tisbury

Bristol Channel

Salisbury

W E S S E X

Plymouth

Map of Chilmark, Wiltshire.

List of Illustrations

Introduction

Two villages; one name; separated by an ocean. The one, in a Wiltshire valley; the other, on an island off the southern shores of Massachusetts. It seemed there would be two stories to relate of interest to the villages – each to the other – only because of a remote seventeenth-century connection. In the event it proved otherwise: the variations were on the same or similar themes, and the influences that shaped people's lives had common origins.

The main historical happenings in both countries have been outlined in order to create a framework for the lives of the communities. Although the rural surroundings might suggest that most lives were relatively uneventful, they were not free of hardship and danger and were often led against a background of strife – when Danes, for instance, hammered Saxons or when French and Indians raided New England colonists. The connection between these two villages ended tragically when, in the Revolutionary War of Independence, the British raided the island of Martha's Vineyard and all but destroyed its economy.

Most of all, this is the story of the family who transplanted the names of Chilmark and Tisbury to the New World, who shaped the early history of the settlers on Martha's Vineyard and who, by their honourable dealings and sense of mission, were exemplary in their relationships with the native Americans.

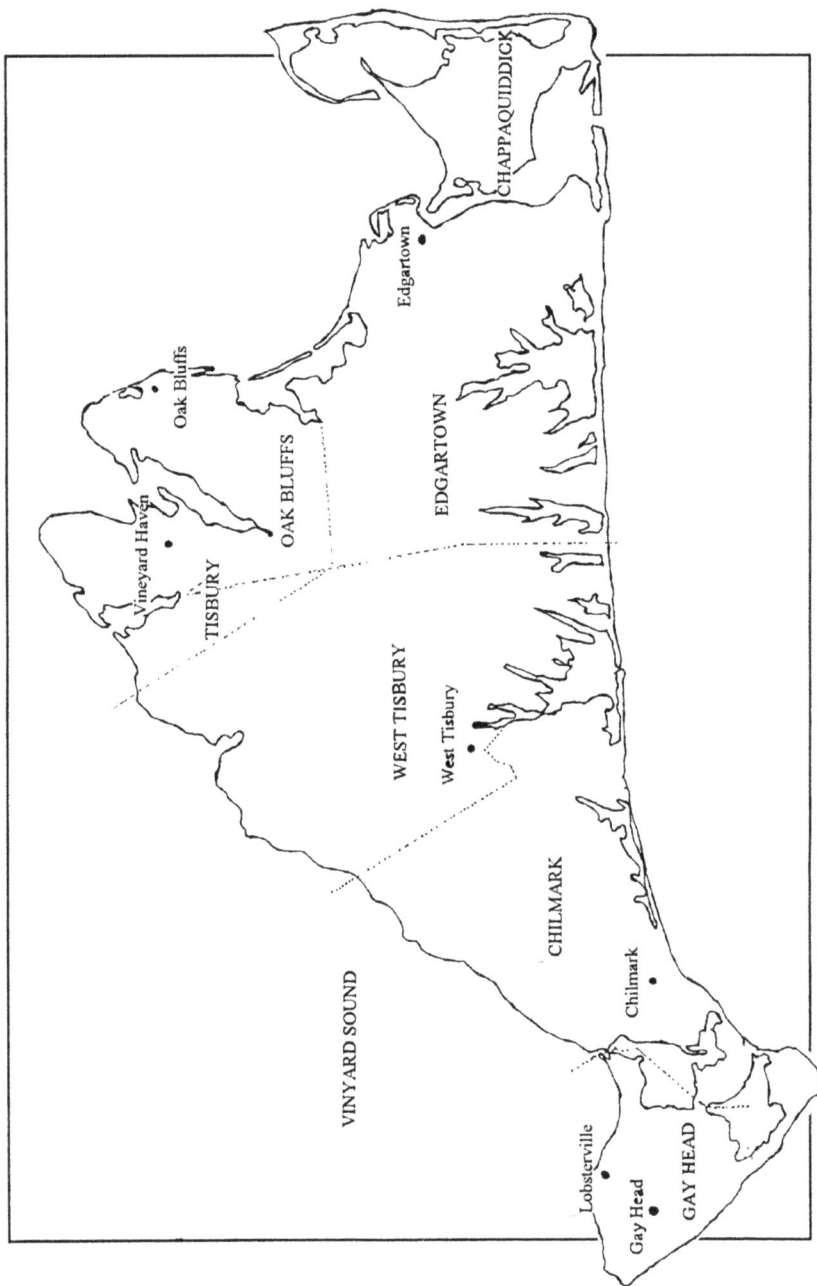

Map of Chilmark, Martha's Vineyard.

Chapter 1

THE LINK

Thomas Mayhew: 1593–1683

A MAN WHO TRADED in 'Beds and Boulsters and Mattress Tikeing' may seem an improbably prosaic description for the most important man in our story – but Thomas Mayhew was such a man. He it was who bought the development rights to the island of Martha's Vineyard and gave the names of his birthplace, Tisbury, and its neighbouring village, Chilmark – both in Wiltshire, England – to two of the townships he founded on the island.

The Mayhew family were yeoman (land-owning) farmers, who came originally from Dinton (4 miles from Chilmark), but Thomas's grandfather, also Thomas, was one of five brothers who spread into several more villages in the Nadder valley: one, Walter, went to Chilmark and Thomas himself went to Tisbury. This Thomas had a son, Matthew, who was the father of another Thomas – the settler and first Governor of Martha's Vineyard.

We know little of young Thomas's early life. A few facts and dates emerge: that he was baptised in the church of St John the Baptist, Tisbury, in April 1593; that, as a boy, he was apprenticed in Southampton as a mercer (dealer in fabrics) to his cousin Richard Macy from Chilmark; and that, when he was twenty-one, his father died, leaving him £40 of 'Good and lawfull Monie of England'. This was to be paid to him at a rate of £4 per annum – not an 'independence' but a useful addition to his income. Certainly he must have felt financially secure when, five years later, he married and had a son – yet another Thomas. This Thomas was to become an important person in the history of the Vineyard and a legendary Christian missionary among the Wampanoag Indians of the island (see chapter 7).

Perhaps trade in 'Beds and Boulsters and Mattress Tikeing' did not prosper or perhaps the grass of the New World looked greener (or, more probably, the sea looked bluer) – or perhaps, best of all reasons, Thomas and his family were inspired with a sense of adventure. Religious adherence may have been a factor: the Tisbury Mayhews were Church of England (Episcopalians), but in order to join the exclusively Puritan colony of Massachusetts Thomas must by this time have been a Puritan himself. In any event, in 1630, Thomas sailed to New England to act as agent for a London merchant, Matthew Craddock, formerly governor and still a powerful influence in the new Massachusetts Bay Company. With him sailed his son, Thomas (now ten years old), and possibly his wife – although it is uncertain if she was alive at this date.

The Mayhews lived in a 'greate Stone House' at Medford, in Massachusetts, originally built for Matthew Craddock, which must have reminded Thomas of the stone houses of his native Wiltshire. Three years later he married his second wife – the widow of a London merchant, Jane Paine – who brought with her two children, Thomas and Jane. The younger Jane married Thomas Jnr in 1647 – so two Thomas Mayhews, father and son, married two Jane Paines, mother and daughter. With two names shared by four of the five family members life must often have been confusing. The elder Thomas and Jane had four more daughters, the last of whom seems to have been called after the Vineyard – Martha.

Thomas Snr was a respected and trusted member of the community and held a number of administrative positions, but his business life did not prosper: in London Matthew Craddock, his fears perhaps exaggerated by distance, wrote of the 'greyffe' he had been 'putt to by the most vyle bad dealings of Thomas Mayhew'. Thomas, it seems, had set up in business with the governor's son when he should have been devoting himself exclusively to Craddock's interests. He lost his job as Craddock's agent and removed to Watertown, where he purchased land and was part-owner of a mill – but still 'it pleased God to frown upon him in his Outward Estate'. His life's work was not to be among mills any more than 'Beds and Boulsters'.

It was then, in 1641, that the opportunity came to acquire the rights to develop land on Martha's Vineyard. At this time the island was not part of Massachusetts but had two English claimants. One was William Alexander, Earl of Stirling – Lord Proprietor of Long Island and other mainland territory; the other was Sir Ferdinando Gorges, Lord Proprietor of the Province of Maine and the 'Isles of Capowack [the collective name for the Indians of the Vineyard] and Nautican [Nantucket] near unto Cape Cod'. Both men had agents acting on their behalf and, 'to make assurance doubly sure', Thomas Mayhew secured the rights from Lord Stirling's agent to 'plant and inhabit' first Nantucket and the neighbouring islands (for £40) and subsequently 'Martin's Vineyard' and the Elizabeth islands (Martin's was an earlier English name for Martha's) and, two days later, signed a similar agreement with the agent of Sir Ferdinando Gorges. Under the remaining English feudal system, Thomas was to give token annual tribute to both men in recognition of their overlordship. To make assurance *trebly* sure he also bought land from the Indian Wampanoag inhabitants. In 1642 or 1643 Thomas Jnr took up residence but Thomas himself did not move to the island until 1645, perhaps waiting until a house had been prepared for them.

The islands became, in effect, independent and self-governing: both Lord Stirling and Sir Ferdinando died and, with the Civil War and Interregnum in England, their heirs had other preoccupations. In 1663, however, (after the Restoration of the Monarchy) the King's brother, the Duke of York, negotiated to buy the Stirling patents and, the following year, Charles II granted his brother a new patent. This covered the territory of New York, Maine, Long Island and 'allsoe all those severall Islands called or known by the names of Martin's Vineyard and Nantuckes otherwise Nantuckett'. (New York had formerly been New Amsterdam but had been renamed, for the Duke, after its recent capture from the Dutch.)

Having governed Martha's Vineyard since 1641 in splendid isolation, Thomas Mayhew cannot have been altogether pleased by this new arrangement but it was

Sir Ferdinando Gorges (c. 1566–1647), Lord Proprietor of the Province of Maine and the 'Isles of Capowack and Nautican near unto Cape Cod'.

a further six years before he travelled to New York for an interview with the governor of the Duke's Province. He need not have worried: six days later he emerged with the Duke's commission as governor of Martha's Vineyard 'dureing his natural Life', as chief justice of the courts of Martha's Vineyard and Nantucket, and with the title, together with his grandson, Matthew, of Lords of the Manor of Tisbury. (Matthew's father, Thomas Mayhew Jnr, had died at sea in 1657: see chapter 7.) This was a precedent in what is now New England, although there were several existing manors in the Province of New York. The title was in perpetuity to their 'Heyres and Assignes' but demanded annual payment to the duke (or *his* heirs and assigns) of two Barrels of good Merchantable Cod-Fish to be Delivered at the Bridge in this

'Two Barrels of good Merchantable Cod-Fish . . .'.

[New York] City'.*

Thomas Mayhew was now eighty years old, but he settled down to enjoy his manorial privileges. These included annual payments of quit-rents from the local farmers to their Lord of the Manor. Payments varied from '2 good Sheep' to 'a good Chees' to 'one Nutmeg' or, in the case of Matthew's younger brother, John, 'one Mink Skin'. The system lasted, despite objection (and even revolt, leading to fines and imprisonment), until 1691 – after the Duke of York, as King James II, lost his throne and a new Charter of Massachusetts Bay gave jurisdiction over the islands to the colony. Thomas Mayhew's successors to the title tried to preserve their manorial rights and, indeed, the fiction was maintained until Independence but, in 1756, the Proprietors of Tisbury had complained, in writing, of 'Sundry Persons [who] have of late Years Presumed to sett themselves up Lord Proprietors of Land in sd Tisbury', 'causing great Disturbance' and the expenditure of 'much Money and Pretious Time'. In a New World the claim of lordship of the manor was obviously resented when it was not derided.

Governor Thomas Mayhew died in 1683, just before his ninetieth birthday, a man of years and honour – and certainly not to be referred to as a 'Sundry Person'.

*Under the ancient manorial system all land theoretically belonged to the Crown, the rights to which could be sold to powerful landlords and subdivided again to lesser landlords, each of whom in turn paid annual dues (mostly in goods or services) to his overlord.

Chapter 2

HOW IT ALL BEGAN

Pre-History & the Romans: 10,000 BC–AD 410

G IVE OR TAKE a millennium or two, the soil of the two Chilmarks was probably first trodden by man at about the same time. As the ice receded at the end of the last Ice Age (*c.* 10,000 BC) men crossed the (then dry) Bering Straits from Siberia, to spread across the American continent, and from Southern Europe across what would later become the English Channel, to populate the countryside of Britain. We will return to these early American settlers in later chapters. In ancient Britain successive waves of invaders from continental Europe meant an ever-changing population and clashes of cultures.

Of the three prehistoric invaders, Neolithic (New Stone Age) man arrived in *c.* 4000 BC. He was succeeded, *c.* 2000 BC, by Bronze Age man and he, in turn, *c.* 600 BC, by Celtic, Iron Age man. The nomad evolved by degrees to become skilled in farming, in crafts, in trade and in tribal warfare.

Then came the Romans, in AD 43, who lived in villas with ornamental gardens, had their likenesses sculpted in marble, wrote history and poetry and civilisation came to Britain. They also brought their law, surfaced roads (one can still be seen 2 miles north of Chilmark) and central heating. Later Britons forgot this comforting skill and had to re-learn it from across the Atlantic in the twentieth century.

The nomad evolved by degrees to become skilled in farming, in crafts, in trade and in tribal warfare.

The legacy of these differing peoples is all around us: Bronze Age man gave evidence of his occupancy by leaving some tools (two axes and a razor were found early in the twentieth century on high ground above Chilmark) but, most importantly, by completing the astonishing structure, begun by his Stone Age predecessors in about 2800 BC, called Stonehenge. It is only 12 miles from Chilmark, so it is not unreasonable to suppose that our early ancestors were among those conscripted to help in its construction. The larger stones that make up the circle were dragged 20 miles (the smallest of these weighs 7 tons) and the smaller bluestones were brought, probably by raft, from Wales – a distance of over 200 miles. Armed with the most primitive of tools, the builders even formed mortise and tenon joints to fix the lintels to the uprights – and all before Moses led the people of Israel out of the Land of Egypt.

The Bronze Age people also left burial-chamber mounds, called barrows, which housed the mortal remains of their chiefs, with jewellery and weapons to equip them for the next world – or perhaps for their re-entry to this.

The Celtic, Iron Age, people left impressive hill forts, with deeply dug concentric ditches and defended gateways from which they set forth to do battle in their horse-drawn chariots. Tisbury, Teffont and Wylye hill forts are all within 5 miles of Chilmark and, most impressive of all, Old Sarum is 10 miles distant.

The Romans, who settled Chilmark to quarry the stone for their roads and villas, left the remains of a settlement at Ridge, the neighbouring hamlet to Chilmark, and their coins occasionally surface after ploughing. In Chilmark itself, a number of stone coffins have been found that date from the Roman occupation. Some were discovered as recently as 1990 – their east-west orientation showing

Armed with the most primitive of tools, the builders formed mortise and tenon joints to fix the lintels to the uprights.

them to be the graves of Christians. The group included four skeletons within stone coffins and, a little apart, that of an infant aged less than six months. Unusually, since the high rate of infant mortality made such care exceptional, the child was also buried in a stone coffin – a loving tribute that touches us across the intervening near two thousand years.

When the Roman Empire collapsed the legions withdrew, along the roads surfaced with Chilmark stone, to try (in vain) to stem the tide of barbarian raids on Rome itself. In the later years they had introduced Christianity to Britain but this, like much else, was largely forgotten. (Nevertheless, Salisbury Museum in the Cathedral Close, has a statue of a Roman centurion and, beneath, a tribute to the Romans in gratitude for their civilizing influence.) With the Romans' departure the unity imposed by their rule fragmented and the ancient Britons, in tribal groupings, fought to establish supremacy and to oppose the next invading force – the Saxons.

Chapter 3

. . . AND CONTINUED

Saxons & Danes: AD *410–1066*

THE STONE, Bronze and Iron Ages ended with the Romans –
whose age was seen metaphorically, and with hindsight, as
'golden'. Saxon England reversed the process to enter the 'Dark
Ages'.

The Angles, Saxons and Jutes (known collectively as the Anglo-
Saxons) first arrived as mercenaries when the Romans departed, in AD
410. They came by invitation of one or other warring faction and stayed
to conquer the land. The Angles colonised the east coast, the Saxons
and Jutes the south – and the Saxons moved west. Here, however,
was the area of most effective opposition, and Chilmark must often
have been near the frontier between the Saxon-held south and the
Celtic west. King Arthur was one of those who kept the Saxons at bay
through the fifth and sixth centuries. He may have been a Roman (his
name, Arturus, the bear, suggests this) or he may have been a Celt,
with or without Roman blood. He may have been a Christian. Sadly,
he was probably little like the paragon of chivalry that later legend
portrays.

When the Saxons finally triumphed the people of Chilmark
must have hoped to pursue their lives, plough their fields and hew
their stone in peace – the two sources of wealth that sustained the
village throughout the centuries. They would have learned to speak

Old English – the Germanic language brought by the Anglo-Saxons – and it was the Saxons who gave Chilmark its name. This is thought to have come from either 'cild' (a child) or, more probably, 'cigel' (a pole or peg), and 'mearc' (a boundary), 'Boundary Pole' may not have been poetic, but it usefully combined description with direction.

The scribes who wrote the *Anglo-Saxon Chronicle* give us glimpses of the events, thoughts and fears in the lives of the people: the Cigelmearcians would have been a superstitious people who watched the skies, not only to forecast the weather for their crops but to look for portents and omens, comets and eclipses. These could presage great events: in the year 685, for instance, 'it rained blood, and milk and butter were turned to blood' – perhaps because 'this same year King Ecfrith was slain'.

Christianity was probably still adhered to in small communities throughout the country, despite the rule of the initially heathen Saxons. One such centre of Christianity was Glastonbury, 40 miles from Chilmark, and perhaps Christians remained in Chilmark itself – with memories supplemented by missionaries who returned to Britain 200 years after the Romans left.

England was divided into four main kingdoms. Chilmark was in Wessex, in the south-west of the country. Rulers of these disunited kingdoms, in the intervals of seeking to defend their borders, applied themselves to building monasteries and abbeys to promote learning, to care for the sick and the traveller – and to pray for the souls of their founders. In the ninth century Alfred the Great, King of Wessex, built the Abbey of Shaftesbury (replacing an earlier foundation in Tisbury) and installed his daughter, Æthelgifu, as the first abbess. He also founded an abbey at Wilton, adding to an existing priory, in AD 890. This abbey became the owner, through the gift of King Athelstan in the tenth century, of the village of Chilmark.

Wilton Abbey gives Chilmark one of its two connections with sanctity: seventy years after the abbey's foundation King Egbert visited Wilton and there met a nun called Wulfthryth. Wulfthryth was young

Edith held to the view that cleanliness was next to godliness.

and no doubt comely and the consequence was Edith. Wulfthryth later became Abbess of Wilton – and Edith became a saint. Edith held to the view that cleanliness was next to godliness, and when St Adelwold reproved her for wearing fine clothes, she retorted that in her 'garments of gold thread' she could be as virtuous as he was 'in his filthy skins'.

One of the benefits of Christianity was the certainties it provided, not only for the world to come but also relating to man's place in an ordered past. Christians knew beyond doubt that in AD 800 the world was exactly 6000 years old. With equal conviction they held that the early Saxon kings' ancestry could be traced, by direct descent, through Cerdic (the first Saxon King of Wessex) to Adam and Eve. It was something to put in the balance against portents and pestilence, occasional famine and the brutalities of war.

The greatest affliction that befell Saxon England was the next wave of invaders, the Vikings. The Norwegian Vikings raided, burned and looted the north and west (from the eighth century onwards) and the Danes later terrorised the south and east. At the same time the northern Vikings, from their bases in Iceland and Greenland, raided the eastern seaboard of North America. They almost certainly set foot in New England and may well have landed on Martha's Vineyard (see chapter 5). There is no evidence that the Danes marched through the English Chilmark – although in 871 King Alfred fought an invading Danish force at Wilton. Seven years later he gained a decisive victory over the Danes. Their king, Guthrum, was converted to Christianity and thereafter the country was divided, by agreement, between Alfred's Wessex and Guthrum's 'Danelaw'. Alfred was able, learned and pious. He established an effective navy to counter the Danes at sea, and his defeat of them probably saved Anglo-Saxon culture from extinction. It is unfair, therefore, that he should be best remembered for burning cakes! Just as the Celts, under Arthur and others, had held back the invading Saxons from conquering westwards, so King Alfred of Wessex prevented the invading Danes from over-running the west – but this cannot have made life comfortable for Chilmark's ancestors, who were constantly near the scene of battle.

If Alfred was the most successful of the Saxon kings, Ethelred was the most disastrous – always 'unready' for the next Danish marauding raid, as they swept through the country destroying it 'by fire and the edge of the sword'. In one raid, in 1002, they sacked and burnt Wilton after the local levies – which might well have included men from Chilmark – were deserted by their leader, Ealdorman Ælfric. He indulged in a vivid pantomime of being taken sick, which convinced no-one, and his faint-heartedness infected the rest. After 100 years and more of plunder, pillage and extortion the people were demoralised.

When Ethelred died the Saxons, wearied by the struggle, accepted the Danish Canute as their king. He married Ethelred's widow, Ælfgifu, also known as Emma, who then became the mother of a Danish son (the next king, Hardicanute) as well as a Saxon son (his successor, King Edward the Confessor). She was a Norman – the sister of Duke Richard II of Normandy, the grandfather of the next, and last, invader – William the Conqueror. If 'the hand that rocks the cradle is the hand that rules the world', Ælfgifu held a deal of power in her grasp.

If 'the hand that rocks the cradle is the hand that rules the world', Ælfgifu held a deal of power in her grasp.

Chapter 4

. . . AND DEVELOPED

Normans to Tudors: AD 1066–1600

THE NEW Norman rulers were of Viking stock, having come to Normandy five generations earlier. The first duke, Gongu Hrolf, or Hrolf the Walker (so called because no horse could carry his vast weight), had seized the rich farmland of northern France as a base for consolidating and extending Norman power.

One of William the Conqueror's most important acts, after establishing control of England, was to commission the Domesday Book – to establish just what it was that he had conquered. He would have read for the entry on Chilmark:

> The church itself [i.e. Wilton Abbey] holds CHILMERC.
> In the time of King Edward [the Confessor] it paid geld for 20 hides [*c.* 3000 acres].

The mill at Chicksgrove is described as belonging to Chilmark, and the entry goes on to describe the division of the land into meadow, thorn and pasture. It concludes: 'It was worth £14; it is now worth £15.' This refers to the annual dues payable to the Abbey.

Of William himself, his supporters said that 'Though stern beyond measure to those who opposed his will, he was kind to those good men who loved God.' It is nice to know that, among his endowments to the Church 'for the good of his soul', was one to Wilton Abbey – which had been embellished not long before by King Canute with a shrine to the saintly Edith.

We can only imagine how the people of Chilmark fared through these changes. The people were better off under strong kings, provided they were reasonably just. Weak kings failed to keep their vassals in check – which led to serious abuses. In 1137, for example, the scribes reported that, in order to extort riches, men were tortured by being stretched, crushed or smoked in castle dungeons throughout the land – until the populace 'said openly that Christ and his Saints slept'. Magna Carta, ever since seen as the basis of all Anglo-Saxon freedoms, was the early thirteenth-century agreement that sought to curb the powers of an unjust monarch. More importantly, the possibility of peaceful, rather than violent, evolution was established.

In the thirteenth century the fortunes of the village were enhanced when Salisbury Cathedral was built – of Chilmark stone. Its soaring Early English style was a triumph of medieval engineering and artistry. The first Salisbury Cathedral had been built, soon after the Conquest, alongside a Norman castle on the old Iron Age hill fort of Old Sarum but was abandoned when the priests objected that the boisterous behaviour of the soldiery in the castle disturbed their devotions. The spire of the new cathedral, the tallest in the country, was added a century later. Maintenance of this 400ft spire, not part of the original plan and standing on a mere 4ft foundation, has challenged the ingenuity of architects and engineers ever since. It remains a landmark – and a source of inspiration to poets, artists and the people of the surrounding countryside alike. Among its many treasures the cathedral holds, and displays, one of the four existing original copies of Magna Carta.

Until the thirteenth century Chilmark would have had a succession of wooden churches, very likely on the site of the present church – and themselves most probably on the site of an earlier pagan shrine. A cross would have stood in the centre of the village (on a site still called The Cross) as a meeting-point, for the exchange of wares, and as the place where villagers listened to the itinerant friars who came to preach from time to time. What is thought to be the base of this medieval cross now stands in the churchyard.

At the end of the twelfth century Chilmark was to have its own stone church. It was cruciform in shape, with a simple and gracefully arched central crossing supporting the tower. The lancet windows in the chancel, the priest's doorway and the endearing stone corbels supporting the chancel roof all date from this period. A hundred years later the porch was added. In those days the porch was the setting for conducting parish business, for the absolution of penitents and for exacting penance from vow-breakers. When marriage vows were broken the wrongdoer had to parade in a fair white sheet, before

The church of St Margaret of Antioch, Chilmark, Wiltshire.

standing in the porch during morning service to show repentance. Many parishes had their own customs: anyone travelling to Dunmow, in Essex, for instance, who knelt in the church porch and swore that he had not quarrelled with his wife nor wished himself unmarried for a year and a day could claim a gammon of bacon – a 'Dunmow Flitch'. (In five centuries only eight people were so rewarded!) The beautifully proportioned spire of Chilmark church was not added until the eighteenth century, the Age of Elegance, and the Victorians contributed the vestry and the north aisle.

St Margaret of Antioch was designated the patron saint of Chilmark church – giving the village its second connection with sanctity. Why she was chosen is not recorded, but it is the kind of dedication that was brought back from the Crusades. St Margaret is an enigmatic figure: she is reputed to have been a 'maiden-martyr', who, according to the *Oxford Dictionary of Saints*, was 'swallowed by a dragon before she was beheaded'. The dragon is said to have 'burst asunder'. Other versions say she was also boiled in oil; yet others suggest that she may not have existed. We can only hope, for her sake, this last was true. However, readers of this tale will be glad to know of St Margaret's promise that those who write or read her history will receive an 'unfading crown in heaven'.

In the Middle Ages, Wilton Abbey continued as owner of Chilmark but, under the Norman feudal system the abbess held the rank and had the rights and duties of a baron. In consequence she was Lord of those Manors, including Chilmark, that belonged to the foundation and, as such, had to supply knights (or payment in lieu) to the king in time of war. The number of knights varied from one to five over the years. It was the title of Lord of the Manor that Thomas Mayhew tried to transplant to the New World in the seventeenth century and which his fellow-islanders considered so inappropriate. The abbess was also patron of the churches under her jurisdiction. As her first appointment to Chilmark, in 1302, she installed one John of Floriaco as the priest.

St Margaret was 'swallowed by a dragon before she was beheaded'.

Another John – John of Chilmark – was renowned in Oxford in about 1386 as a philosopher and mathematician, and was known as the Archimedes of his day.

Wessex was a relative backwater in the Middle Ages, partly because, with a single English kingdom, the centre of government had removed from the Saxon capital of Wessex, Winchester, to London. The Black Death of 1348 is not known to have reached Chilmark itself, although it certainly raged further north in Wiltshire. In the country as a whole, one third of the population was wiped out by the plague and, thanks to subsequent outbreaks, it halved again between the fourteenth and fifteenth centuries. During this time Wilton Abbey, Chilmark's landlord, from being the richest in the country, was progressively impoverished and was often in debt. It was in this state, and with its buildings in disrepair, when Henry VIII dissolved the monasteries – together with the abbeys, priories and friaries – in 1539.

English schoolchildren (and often their elders) tend to confuse whether it was Henry VI who had eight wives or Henry VIII who had six. It was, of course, the latter. Whatever Henry's standing as a monarch, it is fair to conclude that, as a husband, he would not have qualified for a 'Dunmow Flitch'. It was the Pope's refusal to grant Henry VIII a divorce – to marry the second of his wives, Anne Boleyn – that was the spark that led to the king's break with Rome and the founding of the Church of England – but it coincided with the reforming Protestant movement that was sweeping through northern Europe at this time.

Anne Boleyn has a minor connection with our story when she tried to install a relation of hers, one Eleanor Carey, as Abbess of Wilton instead of the candidate elected by the nuns. 'Serious moral charges' were, however, brought against Eleanor, and Anne was overruled. 'Serious moral charges' were, of course, later brought against Anne herself, for which she lost her head in 1536. Three years later, at the Dissolution of the Monasteries, when Wilton Abbey surrendered, the abbess was given a pension of £100 a year, a house and a cartload of wood every week – and Chilmark had a new lord of the manor, Sir William Herbert, later Earl of Pembroke.

By the end of the sixteenth century Elizabeth I, the daughter of King Henry and Anne Boleyn, was on the throne of England. The country's population had again doubled, leading to a shortage of land, and men were looking to the New World in which to expand. At the same time Henry VIII's Church of England had reformed much of the doctrine of the Church of Rome but retained much of its ritual. The new doctrine was unacceptable to the Roman Catholics while the old ritual and, in particular, the retention of bishops and the 'rags of popery' (vestments) were unacceptable to the Puritans. Some of the former, led by Lord Baltimore and his wife Anne Arundell, whose family were lords of the manor of Tisbury, were to leave to found the colony of Maryland; many of the latter, led by the Pilgrim Fathers, were to leave for New England.

It was in this England, in 1593, that Matthew Mayhew and his wife Alice had the third of their seven children, and called him Thomas.

Chapter 5

IN THE MEANTIME . . .

Explorers & Settlers: AD 1000–1630

B UT WE NEED to retrace our steps. The Puritan Pilgrim Fathers, who sailed in the *Mayflower*, were not the first to cross the north Atlantic. The most intriguing area of speculation concerns the Vikings and the whereabouts of their sightings, landings and brief settlement of the North American Atlantic coast. The Sagas, which tell of their enterprises, were handed down by word of mouth – and the stories no doubt gained in the telling – before being written down. They are, nevertheless, accepted by historians as based on fact, not mythology – and describe events that had taken place 200 years earlier, at the same time as the Danes were harassing England under Ethelred the Unready.

The two surviving Sagas of the American voyages tell the same story, with some variations, of Eirik the Red, the patriarch of Greenland, and his family. The earlier (Greenland) Saga, which is thought to be the more accurate, describes how an Icelander, called Bjarni Herjolfsson, was blown off course when searching for Greenland and, in about AD 985, sighted what were probably the coasts of Newfoundland, Nova Scotia and New England. He did not land, but his description of these western lands inspired one of Eirik the Red's sons, Leif the Lucky, to set out on a voyage of exploration. He sailed in about 1001, and arrived in a land of wild grapes and wheat, rolling grasslands, massive timber and an abundance of game and fish. He named the country Vinland, after the vines that grew wild along the coast.

Leif was followed by a brother, Thorvald, a brother-in-law, Thorfinn Karlsefni (son of Thord Horse-Head) and an illegitimate sister, Freydis. Thorvald was shot by an Indian arrow and the wound proved fatal. Thorfinn Karlsefni should, perhaps, have been warned by this event but he set out in turn, determined to settle the land, and took with him sixty men, five women and a variety of livestock. His wife gave birth to a son, Snorri, in Vinland – the first American-born European – but despite surviving two winters and initially trading skins for milk with the Indians in a friendly way, their later hostility caused him to abandon his ambitions and return to Greenland. The last of the family, Freydis, was an unattractive warrior who ordered the killing of half the members of her party – and herself killed five women with an axe – in order to appropriate their ship for the return voyage. The second Saga describes how on one occasion, when she was being pursued by some warlike Indians, she turned and smote her bared breast with a sword – at which the Indians were awe-struck into flight. If Freydis's hand ever rocked any cradles, like her contemporary Aelfgifu (Emma), we can only worry for their occupants.

The question remains, where was Vinland? It is generally accepted that it lay between the Hudson and the St Lawrence rivers and was probably somewhere on the New England coast. It may well have been on the southern shores of New England in the area that includes Martha's Vineyard. Perhaps, like all the best mysteries, it is more rewarding to speculate than to arrive at a certainty.

The Viking Empire declined, and in the fifteenth century, after the Turkish Ottoman Empire had blocked the trade routes to Asia, southern explorers like Christopher Columbus began to look west in the search for a route to the spices of the East. In this context it was unfortunate that in 240 BC a Greek called Posidonius got his sums wrong. The result was that the circumference of the world was thought to be a few thousand miles less than it actually is. The missing area was,

Freydis was an unattractive warrior, who ordered the killing of half the members of her party – and herself killed five women with an axe.

of course, the continent of the Americas, but the miscalculation accounts for Columbus's thinking that he had reached the shores of India when he had landed in the West Indies, and for those early explorers who thought they had 'found' a New World. It was not, of course, lost: it was just that Posidonius had mislaid it. Had the (more correctly termed) 'native Americans' been asked (or, indeed, the Vikings), they could have explained that there was nothing so very New about their World – and they could have been saved from the misnomer 'Indians', with which, until recent times, they have had to contend.

It was not until Magellan found the south-west route to the Pacific that the realisation came that the world's oceans were connected, and later still that the land mass of South America was a continent and not the eastern shores of India. From that time the search for gold was uppermost in men's minds, as the Spanish scoured the lands of South America.

The northern Europeans, French, Dutch and English, were content, in the sixteenth century, to roam the seas in pursuit of the riches of Spanish shipping but, towards the end of the sixteenth century, they too began to explore. It was in the search for a north-west, as opposed to Magellan's south-west, passage to Asia that they 'discovered' North America.

The first to sail the length of the east coast of North America, in 1524, was Giovanni da Verrazzano, a Florentine in the service of Francois I of France, the contemporary of Henry VIII. He surveyed the coast around the Hudson river and, in deference to his patron, named the land adjoining New York bay Angouleme – the King's birthplace. After leaving New York harbour, Verrazzano sailed 50 leagues towards the east,

> as the coast stretched in that direction and always in sight of it. At length [he] discovered an island of triangular form, about 10 leagues from the mainland, in size about equal to the island of Rhodes, having many hills covered with trees . . .

He named the island Luisa, or Aloysia, in honour of the mother of Francois I, but bad weather prevented his anchoring. Verrazzano had, however, established and recorded the existence of Martha's Vineyard.

In the fourteenth and fifteenth centuries sea charts were made, with an attempt at accuracy, showing ocean routes together with rivers and safe harbours for anchorage. Artistic licence allowed an abundance of monsters and 'windheads', and showed fauna and flora as well as the inhabitants, their dwellings and occupations. Such a map is that of Giovanni Ramusio, dating from 1556 and based on Verrazzano's voyage and the descriptions of a later voyage of Jacques Cartier in 1534. It is a woodcut, full of information as well as a delightful and imaginative riot of sea monsters. Martha's Vineyard is shown as 'Briso', thought to be in mistake for 'Luisa', and the mainland has become New France. The map also seems to show a long line of shoals the length of the coast, with the mass of islands to the east representing Newfoundland.

So far the explorers had not thought of settling the land. There was no sign of gold and, though fishing and trading for furs was increasing, the country itself was rocky and thickly wooded. In 1602, however, an English ship under 'Captaine Bartholowmew Gosnold', a Captain Gilbert 'and diverse other Gentlemen' landed on Nantucket and Martha's Vineyard. (Since being named 'Luisa' the Vineyard had become known as Martin's Vineyard, but Gosnold renamed it, it is thought, after his daughter.) They explored the islands and delighted in the trees, birds and berries and 'a great standing lake of fresh water, neere the sea-side'. Gosnold and his crew made friendly contact with the Indians, traded for skins and sailed on to another island, Cuttyhunk. This he named Elizabeth Island – after another daughter (it is the name now used for the whole group) – and here he built a house, the first European dwelling in New England.

Gosnold did not settle but his initiative was soon renewed, with the financial assistance of a group of merchants headed by our old friend Sir Ferdinando Gorges (later Lord Proprietor of Maine and one of the two claimants of Martha's Vineyard). Four years later Gosnold established Jamestown, in the Colony of Virginia, but, together with many others of the party, died there in 1607. (The first attempt at colonising Virginia had been made twenty-two years earlier by Sir Walter Raleigh and the land named after Elizabeth I, the 'Virgin Queen'.)

The next endeavour was to seek and secure a second viable trading colony, which was initially named North Virginia. Descriptions of the Cape Cod area attracted the Pilgrim Fathers, who landed at New Plymouth in 1620, and the second, northern, colony grew from their beginnings. The Massachusetts Bay Company was established

A detail from Giovanni Ramusio's map of 1556. (courtesy of the American Museum in Britain)

by Puritan merchants, rather than pilgrims, and given its royal charter (setting out its rights and privileges) by King Charles I. (The Massachusetts Bay Company charter, dated 4 March 1629, granted the company rights to all natural resources of the land but, in accordance with feudal custom, was required to pay the '5th part of the ore of gold and silver found in the territory' instead of 'knight's service' to the Crown. The king had a bad bargain in the event, and might have done better to settle, like his son the Duke of York, for barrels of cod fish – see chapter 1.)

The merchants who first came to form the colony were for the most part Presbyterians, while the Pilgrim Fathers were of the Congregational Church. The differences were mostly a matter of Church government. The Congregationalists believed in government of the Church by individual congregations; the Presbyterians believed in government by Elders. Both were the original Puritans who, as their name implies, had tried to 'purify' the Church of England of its legacy of Roman Catholic forms of worship.

In 1603, after the death of Queen Elizabeth, a group of 750 Puritan clergy had petitioned the new king, James I, for a number of reforms. With one exception these were all rejected. The one concession, which has some connection with our story, was to agree to the commissioning of a new translation of the Bible – the King James Bible – still seen as one of the treasures of the English language. The king himself translated the psalms, assisted by Sir William Alexander, later Earl of Stirling and a noted scholar and poet. He was the same Lord Stirling who became Lord Proprietor of Long Island and (in competition with Sir Ferdinando Gorges) of Martha's Vineyard.

As the Puritans became more vociferous there were attempts to suppress them, and some were tried and sentenced in an attempt to eradicate unwelcome political or religious criticism. Punishments, or methods of extracting evidence, included torture and mutilation – often branding and cutting off offenders' ears – the latter being the favoured punishment for such offences as 'seditious libel'. It was a policy that persuaded many moderate men to take up the Puritan cause and, in the case of the Massachusetts settlers, to form a theocratic state of their own devising, where they could be free to worship as they wished.

The first governor of the Massachusetts Bay Company, Matthew Craddock, had himself led a party of 200 settlers (and 100 head of cattle), but realising, perhaps, that he was not of the stuff of which colonial pioneers were made, returned to England. Craddock continued to supervise the company's affairs from London but, at his suggestion, it was decided that it should be governed from Massachusetts and not, as was usual, from England – in order to distance it from the king's tax-collectors. The Puritan John Winthrop was appointed governor of the colony, as well as the company, and helped to establish the spirit of independence for which New England was later noted. At the same time Craddock appointed an agent to represent his interests and supervise his private estate at Medford. After a year, however, the agent, Philip Ratcliffe, was accused of 'most foul, scandalous invectives against our Churches and Government', for which he was banished, whipped – and had his ears cut off. The early English settlers, who had known religious discord, had no intention of letting factions develop that would jeopardise their new-found unity of purpose.

The post of agent to Craddock was now vacant – and Thomas Mayhew accepted the challenge.

Chapter 6

THE MEETING-GROUND

Indians & Englishmen: AD 1600–1675

I N CHAPTER 2 we left the prehistoric American settlers spreading across the North American continent – the men hunting and the women gathering. It is not known exactly when they first set foot on Martha's Vineyard, but they were established on the island circa 3000 BC – about the same time as Neolithic man was beginning Stonehenge and 1000 years before Bronze Age man first left his tools in the English Chilmark.

We caught a glimpse of these native Americans during the Viking raids, in the eleventh century, but otherwise their development between 3000 BC and the sixteenth century is conjectural. We can imagine, however, that the rich hunting and fishing shores of Massachusetts would have been particularly prized. Certainly by the sixteenth century the hunter-gatherers had become settled farmers, as well as still exercising their ancient hunting skills – which had been developed to include awe-inspiring sea-going expeditions to spear whales in nothing more substantial than dug-out canoes (see chapter 9). The Wampanoags, meaning 'easterners', were part of the Algonquin linguistic group (whose territory covered a vast swathe of the eastern sea-board of North America and the area round the Great Lakes, westward). A tall, fair-skinned and dignified people, they lived within a form of feudal society with a hereditary nobility. The main

Dug-out canoes illustrated in a contemporary print.

groupings were the sachemships, each sachem (not unlike a Lord of the Manor) owing allegiance, through a hierarchy, to the Great Sachem, or king. Martha's Vineyard had four sachems: of the Chappaquiddicks in the east, the Nunnepoags at Edgartown, the Takkemmys in mid-island, and the Aquinnahs, of Gay Head and Chilmark, in the west.

In 1611, nine years after Gosnold's exploration of the island and nine years before the arrival of the Pilgrim Fathers, another expedition landed and captured a young Indian called Epinowe. He and four others (three from the mainland) were taken back to England, where Sir Ferdinando Gorges (again) took three of the five into his charge. (It should be explained that Sir Ferdinando, who has been called the 'Father of English Colonisation in America', was the governor of Plymouth, England, which is why he always seemed to be in the right place at the right time. Many ships would have left, and returned, there when crossing the Atlantic.) Sir Ferdinando was under the impression that it was not possible to teach these unwilling members of his household: it was said that Epinowe 'could say "welcome, welcome", this being the last and best use they could make of him'. They were proved wrong after Sir Ferdinando was persuaded by Epinowe (whose English must by this time have improved) that there was gold on the Vineyard. Sir Ferdinando immediately fitted out a ship and sent an expedition to the island, with Epinowe aboard to act as guide. We must assume that the glint of gold overrode natural caution: the ship crossed the Atlantic without mishap, anchored off Martha's Vineyard – and Epinowe escaped under the protection of a hail of arrows delivered by his friends and relations.

Nothing daunted, Sir Ferdinando equipped another ship under a Captain Dermer. This ship stopped twice at the Vineyard, on the outward and return journeys to Virginia. The first visit was friendly but the second ended in disaster. Epinowe had been laughingly recounting his earlier escape but, on discovering Dermer's identity, feared he was about to be recaptured. In the fight that ensued Dermer was badly wounded. He fled to Virginia but died there – either of

Epinowe escaped under the protection of a hail of arrows delivered by his friends and relations.

sickness or of the 'fourteen wounds' he sustained in the fight. It was the last time there was any violence between Indian and European on Martha's Vineyard – and it was the Mayhew family who, by setting a standard of fair dealing, were very largely responsible for such an exemplary state of affairs.

The same was tragically not always true of the mainland. The first settlers had been greeted with kindness by the chief sachem, Massasoit, who had helped most of them to survive the first hostile winter – teaching them the Indian's skills in farming and trapping and introduced them to growing maize. The tragedy arose from two main causes: the first was the introduction of diseases to which the Indians had no resistance – smallpox, measles, tuberculosis and even the common cold were usually fatal – and wiped out whole families, and often communities, at a time. The second was the treatment of the Indians by the settlers themselves. As their numbers grew the pressure upon the land increased, and not all were as scrupulous in their dealings as Thomas Mayhew. Inevitably, among their number were those who felt impelled to demonstrate their mastery over what they saw as a heathen race. It was a time when 'the Lord's doing' was perceived in every eventuality. It was thus 'the Lord's doing' that the settlers had crossed the seas, made a safe landfall and prospered on foreign soil. By the same token, when the Indians died in increasing numbers it was seen as the Lord's judgement on an ungodly people. Under this influence the Indians began to see things in the same way: at a court hearing over a land dispute in 1643, when asked if they would worship the true God, they answered that 'We desire to speak reverently of the Englishmen's God and not to speak evil of Him, because we see the Englishmen's God doeth better for them than other Gods do for others.' With hindsight we may weep, but the settler's attitude was part of the received wisdom of the time. It was another hundred years before it was acceptable for Benjamin Franklin to introduce his invention of the lightning conductor, which earlier would have been seen to be diverting the Lord's just punishment of a sinner.

When the gentle and welcoming Massasoit died his two sons, Wamsutta and Metacom, whom the classically educated settlers called Alexander and Philip (after Alexander the Great and his father, Philip of Macedonia) followed in succession. It was the younger son who decided to make a stand. Philip recognised that the two cultures could not coexist, and determined to send the Anglo-Saxon invaders back whence they came. Perhaps there was a folk-memory of expelling the Vikings from these shores in the eleventh century, and the Indians hoped that history could be repeated.

King Philip's War broke out in 1675, with a confederacy of tribes forming a combined attacking force. Not all the Wampanoags, however, joined the fight. The very success the Mayhews and others had had in establishing a harmonious and trusting relationship with the indigenous people on Martha's Vineyard resulted in the island sachem's refusal to obey the chief sachem's summons. Victory, nonetheless, must always have been a forlorn hope, and when King Philip was killed the heart went out of the resistance.

Before returning briefly to England, to see how Chilmark fared in the English Civil War, perhaps it is worth considering the extent to which, throughout history, the vanquished in any conflict left a legacy of wisdom and influence. This is true of the Indians – the native Americans. It had also been true in England, where the succeeding cultures all left their mark: Celtic, Roman, Saxon, Danish or Norman. Even Stone and Bronze Age men's combined efforts gave us Stonehenge – to baffle our understanding and command our respect.

Chapter 7

HERE AND THERE

Puritans & Missionaries: AD 1640–1670

THE PURITAN EXPERIENCE in England took a very different course from that in Massachusetts, although its origins were the same. The Stuart kings believed in monarchy as a sacred trust, which they exercised by 'divine right'. It was the royal version of 'the Lord's doing' by which all men understood their lives to be governed. Few disputed the principle but its interpretation – that the king's judgement could not be challenged – was the source of wide-ranging opposition on religious, political or legal grounds. The tensions exploded in the Civil Wars of 1642–5 and 1647–8, when Royalist, Cavalier dash and enthusiasm crossed swords (and muskets) with Parliamentary, Puritan zeal and discipline. Mainly at issue was whether king or parliament governed the country. The Parliamentary 'Roundheads' (so-called because they wore their hair short, unlike the flowing locks of the Cavaliers) controlled London and hence had access to greater wealth. This, coupled with the greater military skill of their New Model Army, eventually gained the Roundheads their victory.

The Puritans in New England who might, like Thomas Mayhew, have left England only twelve years before (many much less) were naturally anxious for their friends and families still in England. Their loyalties were with the Puritan forces and some, like Stephen

Winthrop, son of the Massachusetts Bay governor, fought on the Puritan side.

One event that must have stirred the passions of the citizens of Chilmark, in England, and still more of Tisbury, was the siege of Wardour Castle (5 miles from Chilmark and just 2 miles from Tisbury). The home of Lord Arundell, who was away fighting for the king, it was besieged by 1300 Parliamentary troops and defended by his wife, her daughter-in-law, her maids and twenty-five fighting men. They held out for six days before being overcome but, the following year, the castle was retaken. This time, Lord Arundell having being killed in the war, his son led the fighting but destroyed the castle in the process. Like so many castles that were fought over at this time, it has been a ruin ever since, but the fighting was notable for the consideration with which each side treated the other. As a contemporary parson noted, the action was 'famous to posterity both for active and passive valour to the utmost'.

The victors in the war were united only in their opposition to the king, not in their reasons – nor in their aims. This became apparent when the moderates, who wanted only to curb the powers of the Crown, found themselves opposed to the extremists who were Republican. It was now that the Army, led by the latter, purged Parliament of its moderate, Presbyterian, members and the fifty who remained (the 'Rump') voted for the trial of Charles I. He was beheaded in January 1649 – an event that some saw as just but at which his followers despaired – and which many of his enemies deeply regretted.

We know of two incidents by which the parish of Chilmark was affected by the Puritan victory: the first was that the Church of England parson was removed and a Puritan, named Sanger, was installed in his place. The second was that Richard Rickette, 'a poore lame mayned man', who had been, he said, 'impressed, guarded and by fforce caried' to join the king's army asked for, and was granted, financial help from his neighbours – he 'being a woonded man for the service of the parish'.

Richard Rickette, 'a poore lame mayned man'.

It was probably during this time that the statue over the south door to the church was removed. Almost certainly the empty niche would once have held a statue of the patron saint, St Margaret of Antioch (with or without her dragon), but it was the practice of the Roundhead soldiery to destroy images that were perceived as idolatrous or 'popish'. Two thirteenth-century supporting angels at the base of the arch remain, below the empty niche.

For four years after the king's death in 1649 the country was a republic, but this period ended when Oliver Cromwell, the victorious general of the war, disbanded Parliament, assumed the title of lord protector (king in all but name) and later established a much-hated military dictatorship. Cromwell's death in 1659 was the signal for all the differing factions to dispute both the leadership and the direction of events – and anarchy reigned. It was with relief that in 1660

Parliament (its Presbyterian members reinstated) voted for a return to monarchy and the new King, Charles II, was welcomed back – with maypole-dancing (banned under the Puritans), the ringing of church bells and, no doubt, the consumption of much ale. England saw itself as 'merrie' again – and the king matched the mood. Nevertheless, the seeds of liberty of conscience had been sown and many of the Puritan influences lingered.

Wiltshire had always been more royalist in its leanings. A royalist uprising, the Penruddocke (named after the squire of neighbouring Compton Chamberlayne), had taken place five years earlier, when two judges were seized, the sheriff was taken hostage and Penruddocke later lost his head. No doubt, at the Restoration, Chilmark's church bells would have rung out loud and clear.

Two years later, it was proposed to find 'accommodation' between the Presbyterians and the Church of England but the attempt failed, the 1662 prayer book was commissioned to define the Established Church's forms of worship and all remaining Puritan parsons were deprived of their livings. Their last permitted service was an emotional occasion, when one irreverent parishioner named William Lawrence, in a London church, described the occasion when 'much weeping and howling there was . . . I verily believe there was more salt dropped that day from their pious eyes, than would have pickled up all the herrings in the nation'. This was a man who had at least sympathised with the Presbyterians – but most people were weary of great causes. That the village of Chilmark was itself divided in its allegiance is suggested not only by Richard Rickette's claim that he had been taken 'by fforce' to fight for the king in the Civil War but by the meaning behind the name Parson's Pulpit. This is a small piece of ground next to the old post office, which is said to have been the site of services in the seventeenth century. Most probably those who remained faithful to the Puritan cause came to listen to the dispossessed minister – rather than to the reinstated Church of England parson up the hill. (Soon the Puritan ministers were not to be allowed within 5 miles of their former parishes – and any further services were clandestine.)*

And so to Martha's Vineyard and, in particular, Nashowakemmuck which, in the Algonquin language, means 'halfway house' – and which, like 'boundary-pole', means Chilmark.

After Thomas Mayhew's purchase of the development rights of the Vineyard in 1641, his son Thomas Jnr, it will be remembered (see chapter 1), first settled on the island. Thomas Jnr, educated and fluent in Latin and Greek (and with some Hebrew) set about forming a Congregational church in Edgartown, his first home. Described later as a 'bright star', too bright for so small a 'sphere', Thomas was approached by an Indian, Hiacoomes, and in converting this man to Christianity found his vocation. He mastered the Algonquin language and for the rest of his life worked untiringly among his 'praying Indians'.

Soon after Hiacoomes's conversion there was an epidemic on the island – probably another disease brought by the Europeans – and many of the Indian population died. Neither Hiacoomes nor his family, nor, in a later epidemic, other converts were affected – so that it was perceived that the Lord protected His own and further conversions followed. Thomas realised that, as the Indian medicine men (pawpaws) also had a priestly role, so must he have a medical role: his first two patients were cured after prayer but the second of these died, as Thomas had prophesied, after returning to the ministrations

*In a final twist of events the Church of England incumbent, Samuel Leach, was himself replaced, in 1685, by one Thomas Barford. Barford was installed as Chilmark's rector by the new Roman Catholic king, James II (Lord Proprietor of Martha's Vineyard when Duke of York). Barford was one of many priests the king nominated in an attempt to 'Romanise' the Church of England. In the event the king lost his throne, but Thomas Barford survived well into the next, Protestant, reign (of William and Mary). He must have learnt to trim his sails according to the wind of religious change.

of the pawpaw. With the aid of his penknife, Thomas bled the third patient to reduce a fever and fervent prayers of thanksgiving must have been offered when the man recovered. Soon afterwards Hiacoombes was unscathed in his wigwam while a hostile Indian nearby was killed by a bolt of lightning, and when Hiacoombes's wife was safely delivered, after three days of difficult labour, there were further conversions. Nevertheless, one of Hiacoombes' children died in infancy – an event that Thomas used as an example to preach the doctrine of the Resurrection.

If Thomas was the teacher of the Indians, Hiacoomes was their spiritual leader and must have been a remarkable man – both to defy the traditional power of the pawpaws as well as to ignore the derision of his fellow Indians as a 'puppet Englishman', and yet all in a 'sober and moderate spirit'. This was the verdict of a visiting parson from Connecticut on his way to London to report to the Society for the Propagation of the Gospel in New England. The society, first founded at the end of the Civil War, in 1649, had a long association with Martha's Vineyard and gave financial support to Thomas's mission, paying him a small annual salary – initially £20, rising to £40. Later (through a commission in New England acting for the society) they paid £20 *per annum* to Hiacoomes and, admirably mindful of the practical, as well as the spiritual, side of life, gave £40 for imported ironwork, nails and glass for a meeting house (the timber would have been cut locally) and £8 for a boat to cross to the mainland. Still more thoughtful (if inevitably unattainable) was their injunction to Thomas Jnr to encourage his converts to retain their tribal customs and dues. (The Society for the Propagation of the Gospel in New England had been set up by Act of Parliament, at Cromwell's instigation, its missionary and educational work confined to the American Indians. A collection was taken among all the churches in England and Wales, and the money used to purchase, by force, a Royalist property in Norfolk, the rents from which paid the expenses of the Mayhews and others. At the Restoration the society went into abeyance – when the dispossessed family tried to regain their land – but was saved by powerful friends. It was given a new royal charter by Charles II, spreading its work beyond New England to 'the parts adjacent in America' – and the poor head of the dispossessed family got a baronetcy, by way of compensation. The renewed society was, extraordinarily for the time, govemed by a mixture of Church of England and dissenting members, including 'nobility and other persons of quality'. In 1663 the society published a Bible translated into the Boston Algonquin dialect – a copy of which was sent to the king.)

The particular god of the Gay Head and Chilmark Aquinnahs was the giant Moshop, and his wife Squant. He it was who turned Nomansland into an island by drawing his big toe across the barrier reef at Squibnocket Pond, to allow the sea's access. He it was also who, sitting by the shore at Chappaquiddick one day, knocked the ash from his pipe to form the island of Nantucket – and the remains of whose meals are the giant fossil bones found in Gay Head cliffs. The English settlers naturally labelled Moshop the 'Devil' – and one of his works was thus the ledge of rock, the Devil's Bridge, which was Moshop's unfinished attempt at an overland crossing to Cuttyhunk in the Elizabeth islands. In Chilmark there is also a large boulder, known as Moshop's bed, with accompanying, but now fallen, boulster and pillow – which Thomas Mayhew, connoisseur of beds and boulsters, must have enjoyed.

Thomas opened a school for the Indians in 1651, by which time he had 200 converts and the society, again, paid the salary of the schoolmaster. As Arthur Railton, editor of the *Dukes County Intelligencer,* has said: 'it may have been the most costly mission in history, per Indian converted'. Thomas's fame spread to London when articles he had written, aimed at raising more money for the work, were said to be 'full of entertainment, and breathe a most excellent spirit'. It is a happy tribute to one erudite and devout Puritan.

In 1657, together with his brother-in-law, Thomas Paine, and two Indian converts, Thomas set sail for England – a journey that was prompted by the need to sort out Thomas Paine's inheritance in England. Tragically the ship was lost at sea. There is a tradition that the spot where Thomas took his last farewell of his praying Indians, the 'Place by the Wayside' on the Takemmy trail, was forever after commemorated by a cairn – to which a stone was added by each and every passing Indian and where there is now a carved stone memorial.

Thomas left a wife and six children – the eldest of whom, Matthew, was then eleven years old. The Society for the Propagation of the Gospel paid for Matthew's education, together with two Indian boys so that, when grown, he was described as a 'hopeful young man, and hath [the Indian] language p'fectly' – and they continued to support the mission. This was taken over by Thomas Mayhew Snr, now in his sixties, in addition to his other administrative commitments, and in 1670 the first Indian church was built.

In the next generation Hiacoomes's son, Joel, was one of two Indians from Martha's Vineyard who attended the Indian College at the newly completed University of Harvard. In time, Matthew's younger brother, John, took over from his grandfather. He was succeeded by *his* son, Experience Mayhew, and he by *his* son, Jonathan. Jonathan was the most distinguished member of all: born in Chilmark, he left the island as an adult, when his courageous championing of liberal thinking and denunciation of bigotry earned him the description, after the War of Independence, of the 'father of civil and religious liberty in Massachusetts and New England'. It is a remarkable family record.

Chapter 8

LIVING IN THE CHILMARKS

URING Thomas Mayhew's fifteen years in Massachusetts, he saw the settler population grow from a few hundred to over twenty thousand. Moving to the Vineyard in 1645 (paying for his rights in the island with money borrowed against his mill in Watertown), he had found a handful of English – the families of Pease, Vincent, Trapp and Norton were already established – and about fifteen hundred Indians. Reports vary about the latter number and it may have been as high as 3000 – perhaps rapidly reducing after disease took its toll in the early years.

Thomas Mayhew insisted that land purchased from the Native Americans should be paid for and a deed drawn up in both English and the local Algonquin dialect. He was obviously a practical man, if not very astute financially – and two of his transactions give a happy insight into his thinking: he bought a large tract of land from the Indians, in what afterwards became the town of Chilmark in 1688, for 'a cow and a suit of clothes from top to toe and £17 in money'. A similar system operated when he came to sell the development rights to the island of Nantucket (which he had, himself, bought from the Earl of Stirling, in 1641) to his cousin, Thomas Macy, from Chilmark, England, for £30 sterling – and 'two beaver hats, one for my wife and one for myself'. (Mr and Mrs Davy Crockett were never more elegant).

Thomas Macy had come to Massachusetts from Chilmark, England, in the early 1630s (even possibly accompanying Thomas

A large tract of land in what became the town of Chilmark was bought in 1668 for 'a cow and a suit of clothes, from top to toe, and £17 in money'.

Mayhew on the voyage) but may have, according to family tradition, converted to the Quaker faith at that time. This was not tolerated in Massachusetts and he is thought to have been persecuted by his fellow settlers. (Puritan intolerance of other sects was one of the saddest aspects of life among the New English – many having emigrated to escape just such bigotry in England). Thomas Mayhew probably suggested to his cousin that he should move to Nantucket as a refuge – and while both Martha's Vineyard and Nantucket were part of New York Colony – and therefore out of the jurisdiction of Massachusetts. Nantucket was divided between ten landholders, of which Thomas Macy was the first – with Thomas Mayhew retaining a tenth part.

The first land in the Vineyard Chilmark was bought by Thomas Mayhew Jnr but was added to by his father over the years. John Mayhew, second son of Thomas Jnr and congregational minister to both Tisbury and Chilmark, was the first settler to live in Chilmark.

It was in 1671 that Nashowakemmuck was made a town, and later Governor Mayhew called it the 'town of Chilmark in the Manor of Tisbury' – to distinguish it from the town of Tisbury, in the north of the island. Just as in England the parish of Chilmark includes both the village of Chilmark as well as the outlying farms and the small hamlet of Ridge, so the much larger town of Chilmark included the village of Chilmark, the Indian community of Gay Head, the fishing villages of Lobsterville and Menemsha, the area (now part of West Tisbury) of Chickemmoo, the island of Nomans Land and the Elizabeth Islands. Nowadays, Gay Head and the Elizabeth Islands are both separate towns – the latter named the town of Gosnold, after the early explorer.

The many visitors today who come to this Chilmark in the summer would probably claim that it is the most beautiful part of the island, with its hills and valleys, fast-flowing brooks (called rivers, as they would be in England), freshwater ponds and a long and beautiful coastline. The Mayhews and those other early settlers of Chilmark – Allens, Skiffes, Tiltons, Thachers, Bassetts and Hunts – must have been delighted with their new surroundings. Most Europeans visiting the United States for the first time, are overwhelmed by the sheer size and scale of the country. Martha's Vineyard, by contrast, in its compactness, the small scale of its features, the change of landscape over short distances as well as its climate, would have seemed reassuringly similar to the country the settlers had left behind. The main difference, apart from the sea and shore, must have been the mass of trees. William Cobbett, in his *Rural Rides*, wrote of Thomas's native Wiltshire that 'though the downs are naked and cold, the valleys [where all the villages lie] are snugness itself'. There 'the trees are everywhere lofty'. He adds, 'it seems impossible to find a more beautiful and pleasant country than this, or to imagine any life more easy and happy than men might here lead . . .' Thomas Mayhew knew, and probably appreciated, both villages and their settings. Rivals they are not.

The houses were constructed in much the same way as they had been for centuries in England. Two main rooms were built around

The old Mayhew house.

a large central chimney, the larger houses lofted over, where the weaving-loom was kept. Some of the grander houses, like Thomas Mayhew's own, a type known as a 'double whole house', had upstairs bedrooms for his large family. Local, natural, materials were used in the construction: in Wiltshire the houses were stone-built and the roofs thatched with straw: many still are. On the island, stone was abundant in the western, Chilmark, end of the island (from glacial deposits) and did not have to be quarried, but the most plentiful natural material was timber. The Mayhew house, in Edgartown, was entirely stone-built, but usually the lower courses of the houses were of stone, for durability, while the main part of the structure was of timber: pine or oak-framed, clad in shingle or clapboard and with a shingle roof. Again, many still are. There was an additional advantage to this form of building since, if required, it was a relatively simple matter to dismantle the structure and move house – literally – on ox-drawn sledges.

In the early days on the Vineyard there was a shortage of tools for both farm and home, most having to be imported, but the list of household goods of a tailor from Chilmark, England, in 1705, shows that the early settlers were not exchanging a life of ease for one of hardship. Comfort was in short measure in both communities. Our Wiltshire tailor's total worldly goods amounted to four cooking pots, six platters, twelve plates, two table-cloths, one settle, one warming-pan, four pairs of shoes, nine pint or quart pots, two pairs of 'hangrels', fire shovel and tongs, six napkins, two table-boards, two chairs and benches and brewing equipment. Upstairs, were four beds and bedding and four chairs. It is not an extensive list and there is no mention, even, of a knife to eat with but at least, at the end of a long day, there was a fire to sit by, a pint (or quart) of ale for cheer and a warming-pan to take the chill off his bed at night.

As the Vineyard Chilmark developed, so did its community buildings. The first school was probably opened for the Indians – it is thought by Matthew Mayhew – but great debates took place on the siting of a school for the settler children. Including the islands, the community was so widely scattered that argument raged long and furiously as to whether the school should be in Chilmark, or elsewhere, or should be moved from place to place. Unable to resolve this vexed problem, an appeal was sent in 1731 to West Tisbury, asking them to arbitrate – and a committee of Tisbury 'Solomons' gave as their verdict that the school should spend ten months in Chilmark village and two months in Chickemmoo. Paine Mayhew, son of Matthew, was deputed to provide the building, 20ft long by 16ft wide and 6ft 'in the upright and be finished as the sd Mayhew Shall think best and most Convenient for that use'. In the end a smaller building was commissioned – of timber, covered in 'Clabord or shingles' and with a brick chimney, but when this needed repair the town was again indecisive. It was finally minuted ('after a considerable Silance') 'so far as the time remained of the three years as Should be remaining after the time expired that the School master was hired for and then brake up the meeting'. As Dr Banks, author of the nineteenth-century *History of Martha's Vineyard*, comments, 'spelling and confusion of expression like that might break up any meeting . . .'. Educating Chilmark's

The graceful United Methodist church, Chilmark, Martha's Vineyard.

younger citizens continued to exercise the mental elasticity of their elders until, in the nineteenth century, four public schools (one on Nomans Land) were established and their position fixed.

In the English Chilmark, schooling was in the hands of the Church and a 'Dame's school' was held, sometimes in the old Rectory, until in 1860 the Earl of Pembroke, successor to those early abbesses of Wilton, gave the land for the present purpose-built school –constructed of Chilmark stone.

The first meeting house in the Vineyard Chilmark was probably erected in the Rev. John Mayhew's time, *c.* 1700. A succession of timber meeting houses followed on the site of the former village (north-east of its present position) until, at the end of the eighteenth century, the Methodists arrived in Chilmark and later built their graceful classical, columned and pedimented church. Moved to its present site in 1910, it had a spire added to the structure just as, in England, where the spire is a much later addition to the village church.

The English church has already been described (see chapter 4) but something should be said of its bells. There are six of these, hung in the bell tower below the spire. The two oldest are 'Angelus' bells – that is, their inscription reads '*Ave Gracia Plena Dominus Tecum*', which translates as 'Hail, highly favoured, the Lord is with thee' – and almost certainly date from the thirteenth century. There are two seventeenth-century bells, one of which is inscribed 'Ring out the bells in God rejoice. I.W. 1616'. The other had been hung three years earlier. Thomas Mayhew might well have been present when either of these bells was consecrated: his grandfather's brother, Walter Mayhew, a churchwarden of Chilmark church, had died in 1606 but there were near relations in the village. (Thomas did not leave for Massachusetts until 1630.) Finally, two more bells were added in the nineteenth century.

Two of the bells at St Margaret's church, Chilmark, Wiltshire.

By origin, the bells were used from the earliest days of monastic life to call the monks to prayer. Later they were rung for weddings and funerals, at the New Year and on royal occasions. In wartime they are silent but are ordered to be rung as a signal of invasion and to celebrate an armistice. For the funerals of a rector, bellringer or choir-member and on New Year's Eve (for the passing of the old year) the bells are muffled, with leather attached to the clappers, but this is removed at midnight to 'ring in' the New Year with a clarion peel. In the nineteenth century this event was prepared for by taking a collection on Boxing Day, the money being spent by the ringers at the pub, followed by supper and singing at the rectory – and the bell-ringing in church – before, finally, singing 'Auld Lang's Syne' at the village cross. The chances are that this, in Vineyard terms, 'brake up the Meeting'. The New Year is still rung in by Chilmark's bell-ringers, but nowadays (of course) in perfect sobriety.

In former times a 'death' or 'passing' bell was rung to signal a death in the community. Those working in the fields were alerted by a slow tolling of the bell; next there was a count of tolls for the age of the deceased, and finally a 'telling of the sexes': three sets of three rings denoted a man, three sets of two a woman and three sets of one a child.

John Harding (1909–83), organist for fifty-three years and, for a time, captain of the ringers, wrote a book on the Chilmark bells: *Our Bells and the Life Surrounding Them* (from which the notes above are taken). In it he says that, thanks to the number of parish churches throughout the land with bells, 'England became known as the "Ringing Island" for nowhere else could they boast of such peals, so lovely or so numerous.'

Finally there are the chimes, set on the wall in the bell-tower, and the handbells, now often rung by the schoolchildren at village festivities. Mary Webb, in her novel *The Golden Arrow*, describes her fictitious Shropshire handbell ringers playing outdoors at Christmas time – and demonstrating that handbell ringing is no easy skill. They were probably not so very different from their real-life Wiltshire counterparts. One of the ringers, Job Cadwallader, had had trouble controlling his bell:

'I did me best,' said Job; 'but when I'm expecting 'im to waggle he dunna, and as soon as I've giv up expecting he does it sudden-like.'

The Blacksmith gave it as his opinion that Job was master of neither 'his missus nor hisself' so it wasn't likely he'd be master of anything 'as determined as a bell'.

No doubt that evening, too, ended in the equivalent of the Black Dog (which still exists) or the Red Lion or the Bridge Inn (which have gone). In the Vineyard Chilmark both the Puritan nature of its early inhabitants as well as the dedication needed in the setting-up of a new community meant that in 1694 they recorded that they 'thinck it inconvenient to have such houses'. By 1715, however, a licensed inn had been established. The roads were rough and the way arduous for travellers, so perhaps it was demanded by wayfarers rather than the local people.

The Black Dog pub from the churchyard, Chilmark, Wiltshire.

Chapter 9

WORKING IN THE CHILMARKS

S URVIVAL meant hard work; earning a living meant, at best, hard work – and frequently danger. On the Vineyard the settlers farmed in much the same way as they would have done in England, fished and hunted, and developed such manual skills as woodworking and house-building, cobbling and coopering. Often the work was communal – mending fishing nets, for instance – while the women worked together at spinning, weaving and quilt-making. Patchwork – a form of make-do-and-mend – was born of necessity, but turned into a famous, and now much collected, art-form.

Each house would have had its fruit trees and vegetable plot, its chickens and perhaps a pig – later a cow or two and a horse. Both Chilmarks relied for their main wealth on their sheep, the source of meat and wool – and, by folding at night, the means of fertilising the land; while the chickens provided eggs, meat and feathers for bedding. (Maybe Thomas Mayhew brought a supply of mattress 'tikeing' with him to contain the feathers?) In both Chilmarks much of the pasture was held in common and the arable land was divided into strips for cultivation by individuals – rotating the crops from cereal to roots to grazing.

From the earliest days water-powered mills provided a service to the community that lessened the load of subsistence living. In England, Chicksgrove's grist mill was working at least from Saxon times, grinding the corn for Chilmark's bread-makers, and, in the

Both Chilmarks relied for their main wealth on their sheep.

Vineyard Chilmark both a grist mill and a fulling mill (for cleaning and thickening cloth) were established before 1700, making use of the fast-flowing brooks. Later a paint-mill and brick kilns were established on the northern shore of Chilmark and salt works (evaporating the sea water in large tanks laid out above the high water mark) provided a way of preserving meat and fish for the winter. There was a tannery too, and iron ore was mined in the swamps of Chilmark town.

The Vineyard exported timber, fur and salted fish in return for tools, metal articles and glass. In the eighteenth century the list expanded to include luxuries as well as necessities: molasses was one, tea was another – leading to another and more complex story – for another, and final, chapter.

The industry that increasingly came to dominate the islanders' way of life – and make many a fortune – was whaling, while in the English Chilmark the stone quarries were the major employers after farming.

The Chilmark quarries, which had been worked continuously since at least Roman times, provided a high-quality limestone for building and carving. Some of the workings were open-cast but most were mined and the area is pitted with mineshafts, leading down through layers of greensand and purbeck, to the limestone beneath. If we consider that the stone needed for Salisbury Cathedral, alone, is estimated at 75,000 tons and that the process of extracting and working wasted up to 75 per cent, it gives some idea of the size of these vast caverns.

The men worked in the near-dark to extract the blocks of stone – the only light coming from small oil lamps. A number of names can still be discerned, scratched into the oil-smoke-blackened roofs – among them that of Macy, a Chilmark name that came to be well known across the Atlantic, not only on Nantucket but on 34th Street, New York, and in all the big cities of the United States. (The American branch of the family spells the name Macy, the English Macey. Both spellings can be seen in the English Chilmark churchyard. One member of the family, Phillep Macy, who died in 1711, was the village stonemason. His tombstone reads: 'He in his life time engraved stones for many but for himself had no time to engrave any.') In the stone quarries, boys were employed to hold and turn the drills as they were driven into the rock face, after which wedges were hammered into the slots, splitting the rock and bringing the blocks, often as much as 6 tons, to the floor. Not surprisingly accidents were common and, in the Middle Ages, the wounded quarrymen were cared for by the Knights Hospitallers at neighbouring Ansty – who had learnt such arts of medicine as were then known on the Crusades to the Holy Land.

In the eighteenth century, the cutting of the Kennet and Avon canal in north Wiltshire offered cheap transport to other quarries and Chilmark could not compete. Quarrying continued, nevertheless, until the 1930s (using steam-powered compressed-air drills instead of child-held drills), when the site was taken over by the Royal Air Force. Today, stone is still quarried on a small scale, for repairs to Salisbury Cathedral – and the caves are sanctuaries for nine different species of bats.

If working in the dark and dangerous conditions of the quarries demanded powers of endurance, whaling required courage of a different, and very high, order. In the early days on the Vineyard both the Indians, already proficient in the art of whaling and the settlers, who had fished the eastern seaboard long before coming to the country, practised 'shore-whaling'. Lookouts were posted on Prospect Hill (one of the two highest on the island and both at Chilmark) to search the seas for whales. When a sighting was made a double-ended boat, in the case of the settlers, or a dug-out canoe, in the case of the Indians (the Wampanoags did not use birch-bark canoes), would be launched. The Indians used paddles and the settlers used oars as they pursued their prey in the often turbulent waters off the island. The skill needed to steer a small craft in tossing seas, and to harpoon the vast animal as it soared up to 'blow' or plunged below the surface was formidable. The harpoon was attached to a drogue (brake) to tire the whale before it could be lashed to the side of the boat – and the kill was completed with lance or spear. With later, larger, boats, the boat itself was the drogue, leading to the term 'Nantucket sleigh-ride' – surely one of the most exhilarating, and most dangerous, challenges ever devised! Often the boat was overturned, sometimes broken up, or the line had to be severed to prevent both boat and crew being dragged below the surface. Because of their great skill, the man with the harpoon was often an Indian, and one, Amos Smalley, who once killed a white whale, is thought to have been the inspiration behind the story of *Moby Dick*, Herman Melville's epic tale, which vividly records the whalemen's feeling for the grandeur and grace of the whale – which they pursued with fear, respect and something akin to love: 'A gentle joyousness – a mighty mildness of repose in swiftness invested the gliding whale.'

'. . . when you come to sit down before a meat-pie nearly one hundred feet long,
it takes away your appetite . . .'

To quote *Moby Dick* again, 'when you come to sit down before a meat-pie nearly one hundred feet long, it takes away your appetite' so, although the Indians killed for whale-meat, the settlers killed for blubber, replacing their tallow candles with oil lamps. It was not until oil was discovered, just before the American Civil War, that whale oil became outmoded and kerosene came to be used instead. Before then, during the great days of whaling, based on Edgartown, larger, faster ships set off for up to four years at sea, able to process the oil on board and factory ship culling of whales became the norm. However abhorrent such wholesale slaughter may seem to us now, nothing can detract from the courage of those early shore-whaling days, with the six-man crews pitting their skill against a whale that had at least a fighting chance of being victorious.

Once a year work was turned into a festival. In England, the people of Chilmark assembled on Fairmead, next to the church, for the sheep fair, held on the feast day of St Margaret of Antioch, the 20th July, when sheep were bought and sold and when anyone with a skill or product of his handiwork to offer set up his stall. Permission to hold a fair was granted to an individual by the lord of the manor, 'with all tolls, customs, profits, perquisites and benefits whatsoever arising out of them, with liberty to collect them'. In the seventeenth century the Jesse family, whose brass memorial tablet is in the church, held this obviously lucrative benefit. No sheep fairs are held nowadays but the church fete and, in some years, a horticultural show perform something of the same function. Certainly in the case of the former the churchwardens look for all the 'profits, perquisites and benefits' possible to keep the thirteenth-century church in good repair for future generations.

On the Vineyard, the people of Gay Head assembled in a similar way on Cranberry Day – a day appointed by a special 'cranberry officer', elected by the people of the town. On the second day, the Chilmark neighbours were invited to join in and, all who were able, set off on foot or in ox-drawn wagons to pick the wild cranberries that grow in the dunes and bogs of Gay Head. It was a profitable exercise and many a Chilmark kitchen must have had a fine aroma of cranberry as the fruit was prepared for winter use. Cranberry Day, too, became something of a festival and a meeting-place for distant neighbours; perhaps, even, Chilmark couples met or became betrothed on Cranberry Day.

But another sort of marriage was about to be dissolved – as a rumble of discontent with the distant government in London could be heard. Divorce (or independence) was in the air.

Chapter 10

THE PARTING OF THE WAYS

Kith from Kin: 1683–1783

Tʜᴏᴍᴀꜱ Mᴀʏʜᴇᴡ and perhaps his son, Thomas Jnr (who had lived in England until he was ten years old), would have seen themselves as Englishmen, developing English territory overseas. Matthew Mayhew and his brothers – and still more the next generations – must, increasingly, have considered themselves American – and the ties with England, and English values, were of diminishing importance. So it was that, three weeks after his grandfather's death in 1683, Matthew sold the lordship of the manor of Tisbury, alias Chilmark, to Governor Dongan of New York, later Earl of Limerick. Some land went with the title but Matthew retained the greater part himself and, since Dongan was an absentee landlord, acted as his agent. The old system of quit-rents operated and lambs, nutmegs and mink skins continued to be accepted by Matthew on Dongan's behalf. So the matter rested – despite the fact that in 1692 Martha's Vineyard was transferred from the province of New York to the Massachusetts Bay Colony.

With Matthew exercising his grandfather's authority and his brother, John, as minister, the interests of the Indian community were less well safeguarded: Matthew claimed Gay Head as part of the manor – and demanded 'ears of corn' as quit-rents from the Indians, despite their counter-claim that the land was theirs 'forever'. On

Matthew's death, therefore, in 1710, the Society for the Propagation of the Gospel in New England bought the lordship of the manor from Lord Limerick, in order to ensure that the Indians' interests were in good hands – and Gay Head was reserved as Indian territory. That a religious society should take on the title is not so curious, if we remember those nuns of Wilton Abbey who held the manor of the English Chilmark from the eleventh to the sixteenth centuries.

Although recognised as a separate entity by Massachussetts Bay in 1694, Chilmark continued to have what Dr Banks called 'a peculiar legal status' – since there were no owners of land in the usual sense. In 1714, however, the General Court ordered that 'The Mannor of Tisbury commonly called Chilmark' should in future have the powers of all other towns in the province, including the collection of taxes. Arguably the residents of Chilmark might have preferred to continue paying in nutmegs.

If the seventeenth century was most remarkable for the religious fervour that dominated politics and the lives of individuals, the eighteenth century saw the beginnings of a very different way of thinking. Scientific progress suggested that the world was an ordered, harmonious place, where men could believe in a creator of order and harmony; comets were discovered to be on predictable orbits and not harbingers of disaster; the last witches to be condemned were burned, in England, and hanged, in Massachusetts, at this time and sickness, death and disaster were no longer seen as God's wrathful punishment of evildoers. Such thinking brought in new questioning of old assumptions and a sense of living in an enlightened age – with an added sense of man's ability to shape his own destiny. By the same token it suggested to the increasingly frustrated American colonies that they could manage their own affairs very well without dictat from across the Atlantic.

These ideas did not come quickly in New England. The French, who ruled the territory of New France – comprising Quebec and the area around the Great Lakes, southwards – aided and abetted the

Indians in raiding the settlements of Massachusetts and the other New England states. During these French and Indian wars a British standing army was necessary for the peace and security of the citizens. When, however, after the later Seven Years War (which was fought in America as well as Europe), the French lost Quebec and Montreal and the remaining Territories of New France were surrendered, the threat was no longer apparent. The British might claim that the army was there to continue to protect the colonists against the Indians while the colonists themselves saw it as a way of ensuring their compliance with the rule of the British government.

In addition to the standing army, home defence, in both Britain and the American colonies, was in the care of the militia. In Britain, because the standing army was employed extensively in Europe and America – and in New England because of the fear of French incursion – the militia was enlarged during the Seven Years War. Two more companies were added to the Chilmark militia on the Vineyard: the first and second were commanded by Cornelius Bassett and Robert Hatch respectively; the third was an Indian company, commanded by Adonijah Mayhew. Enlarging the force threefold says something of the fears of the time.

Dissatisfaction with British rule came to a head in the 1770s. Chiefly there was the matter of taxes, which were levied to pay for the, now unwelcome, army. The cry of 'no taxation without representation' was taken up – but the British government were slow to read the warning signs. When they did, they gradually removed the taxes except, finally, that of the import duty on tea, as a matter of principle. The concessions were too little and too late.

If the remaining tax on tea was symbolic for the British government of their continued control, it was equally, and unacceptably so, to the colonists. The famous Boston tea-party was the result, when a group of Massachusetts men, disguised as Indians, boarded a ship laden with tea that lay in Boston harbour and threw the chests overboard. As one of several punitive measures a military governor was installed to maintain law and order, and it was an exercise in riot control at Lexington, Massachusetts, that led to the spilling of blood – and the beginnings of first the Declaration and then the Revolutionary War of Independence.

The name Tea Lane in old Chilmark Village dates from the days when it was unpatriotic to drink tea that had paid duty to King George but quite acceptable to drink smuggled tea. The chests were presumably brought ashore and thence along the vine-, blueberry- and huckleberry-bordered Tea Lane to the thirsty and defiant villagers of Chilmark – and where Simon Mayhew, for one, kept his tea under the floorboards in the attic. It was fortunate for Simon that when one day his manservant crept from the house to denounce him to the authorities he was observed – and the tea was hastily removed to a new hiding place.

As an island, the Vineyard's involvement in the war came in a devastating sea-borne attack. Britain's European colonial rivals, France,

Simon Mayhew kept his tea under the floorboards in the attic.

Spain and the Netherlands, happily aided and abetted the American war effort so that the Royal Navy's chief aim was to blockade the American ports – to prevent foreign supplies reaching the colonists. From the British point of view, bringing supplies across the Atlantic was an immense logistical undertaking. American cruisers could, and did, cause a great deal of destruction of British merchant shipping, despite the then superiority of British naval power.

In 1778 France joined America in the war, and the arrival of a French naval squadron forced the British into different naval tactics: the blockade was no longer possible and a plan of 'war by conflagration' was ordered. It was a policy that was carried out half-heartedly. The more far-sighted saw that even if it were possible to destroy every American sea-port it would be to no avail: not only would it destroy that which the British hoped to retain but it would also ensure American hatred in whatever peace transpired. No such thoughts, apparently, troubled the British General Grey who, with an amphibious force, escorted by the frigate *Carysfort*, raided New Bedford, the shores of Buzzard's Bay and Martha's Vineyard – the main objective being to obtain supplies for the garrison in New York.

A near-contemporary British account (*The Naval and Military Memoirs of Great Britain 1772–1783*) describes how, after battling with adverse winds in Vineyard Sound, the fleet came to Holmes' Hole harbour (now Vineyard Haven) to begin 'the business of collecting cattle':

> No sooner did the fleet arrive off the harbour, than the inhabitants sent persons on board to ask the General's intentions with respect to them. He immediately required, that they should deliver to him the arms of the militia, the public money, three hundred oxen, and ten thousand sheep; the two last articles being exactly what they had made a tender of to Congress, for the use of their troops. They promised to send him all these articles, without delay; but he afterwards found it

necessary to order small detachments into the island, and to detain the deputed inhabitants, in order to accelerate their compliance with his demands.

On the 12th [September 1778], some vessels from Rhode Island joined the fleet; on board of which six thousand sheep, and one hundred and thirty cattle, were embarked. The 13th and 14th were employed in embarking cattle on board the transports from New York; in destroying some salt works; in burning or taking what vessels and boats could be found in the neighbouring creeks and inlets; and in receiving the arms of the militia. On the 15th, the fleet sailed for New York.

The account tallies with that given in Colonel Beriah Norton's diary, told from the island's point of view: he describes how, on the fleet's arrival, he 'waited on' the general and agreed to deliver the 10,000 sheep and 300 head of cattle. 'The General informed me that payment would be made if they were not resisted.' On the 11th September the troops landed, under a Colonel Sterling, and the business of collecting and loading the stock began. There is a two-day gap in the diary at this point: it suggests that Colonel Norton was one of those 'deputed inhabitants' whom General Grey found it 'necessary to detain'. On the last day, the 14th, Colonel Sterling repeated to an assembled crowd that they would be reimbursed for the livestock, and that they should apply to New York for payment.

Henry Franklin Norton, in his *Martha's' Vineyard*, tells how, at the outbreak of the war, the islanders agreed to the proposal of one of their number (after first suggesting that he should be hanged for voicing it) that as 'the British come here and pay you good prices for your sheep, cattle and provisions' so it was only sensible to take the money and help their own army in other ways. As this confirms, it seems almost certain that the promise of compensation was made in good faith – but the money was never paid. Henry Franklin Norton writes that a man was sent to New York, and Colonel Norton himself

'On the 15th, the fleet sailed to New York.'

made two trips to London and was given a hearing in Parliament, but 'very little was accomplished'.

The only consolation, if consolation it be, is that it could all have been even worse: on board the transports in the harbour were the Light Infantry, the Grenadiers and the 33rd Regiment, 'because General Grey had a view of employing those corps on a particular service, whilst the business of collecting cattle should be going on upon the island; but contrary winds obliged him to relinquish his designs'. In the days of sail, winds had a habit of frustrating the best – or worst – of plans.

Chilmark suffered the greatest deprivation on the island during Grey's raid: 4000 of their sheep were taken and the tax-collector, Elijah Smith, was deprived of the town's money – and most of his own sheep. (He was later reimbursed by the General Court.) Perhaps it was some comfort to Chilmark that the iron ore from their swamps went to make ammunition for the American war effort.

If taxing tea had aroused a spirit of rebellion, removing half the Vineyard's sheep and cattle aroused the passionate enmity of the whole island. Some had been uncertain how to act at the beginning of the conflict – but their loyalty to the cause of independence was now fixed.

At the same time, British resolution was weakening and with it came the final recognition that the American colonies had come of age. In 1783 peace was signed and independence, won on the battlefields of the New World, was recognised. Exactly 100 years after Governor Thomas Mayhew's death the mutual history had come to an end. From now on, the stories continued on two separate and divergent paths.

The Rev. Jonathan Mayhew.

It seems improbable that Thomas Mayhew could have foreseen the reversal of fortunes of the England he left, which became part of the Great Britain and power of the eighteenth and nineteenth centuries – and the New England he helped to develop, which became part of the United States of America, the superpower of the twentieth and twenty-first centuries. He would have no difficulty today in recognising the Chilmarks: both remain small, rural communities – the island numbers swelled by summer residents. The people, too, although no longer rooted in the land, are aware of their fortune in living in different but unsurpassably beautiful countryside. In considering such men as his descendant, Jonathan Mayhew, perhaps Thomas would have taken quiet pride in the thought that it was the best of the men and women, moulded by the history of the land of the older Chilmark, who were a small seed of influence in helping to build the great nation those American colonies became.

TALE ENDS

1. The activities of the Society for the Propagation of the Gospel in New England were made illegal at the beginning of the American War of Independence. The work was continued in Canada and, later, the West Indies – in both of which (as the New England Company) it still supports schools and missions.

2. The last Indian wigwam disappeared from Chilmark early in the nineteenth century, when its occupants all died of disease (probably smallpox). Today about two hundred people of Indian descent – not all Wampanoag and none of pure Indian origin – live in Gay Head.

3. British and American forces came to blows one more time, in the Napoleonic wars, fought on American soil from 1812 to 1814. Since then, and most importantly in two world wars, they have fought as allies. During the Second World War American troops camped 3 miles from Chilmark, in Groveley Wood (alongside the old Roman road), before the D-Day landings in France.

4. Also during the Second World War, the people of Chilmark, Martha's Vineyard, sent food parcels to the people of Chilmark, Wiltshire – a gesture of kindness and thoughtfulness that was noted in a letter of appreciation, printed in the *Vineyard Gazette*, on 23 January 1948.

5. In 1974 the people of Chilmark, Martha's Vineyard, generously contributed towards the retuning and rehanging of the English

Chilmark's church bells. Such kindness, twice over, is remarkable and suggests a bond of interest that survives the intervening centuries.

6. In 1957 the people of Chilmark, Wiltshire, sent a goodwill document to the people of Chilmark, New England, in the replica *Mayflower* that sailed that year. The reply, signed by a descendant of Thomas Mayhew, hangs in the church of St Margaret of Antioch, Chilmark.

Profits from the sale of this book will go towards the upkeep of Chilmark's 12th-century church of St Margaret of Antioch.

BIBLIOGRAPHY

America in Britain, Vol. XXVII, No. 1, 1989 (The American Museum in Britain) – incl. 'New World, Old Maps – the Adventures of a Collector', Dr Dallas Pratt

Banks, Charles Edward, *A History of Martha's Vineyard* (3 vols) (Dukes County Historical Society, 1966)

Barraclough, Geoffrey (Ed.), *The Times Atlas of World History* (Times Books)

Beaston, Robert, *Naval and Military Memoirs of Great Britain 1772–1783*, 6 vols (Longman. Hurst, Rees and Orme, 1804)

Candler, C.M., *New England Village* (The American Museum in Britain)

Carpenter, W. Boyd, *A Popular History of the Church of England* (John Murray, 1900)

Cobbett, William, *Rural Rides* (Cambridge University Press, 1922)

Craigie, W.A., *The Icelandic Sagas* (Cambridge University Press, 1913)

Oxford Dictionary of National Biography (Oxford University Press)

Douglas David C. and Jensen, Merrill (eds), *English Historical Documents*

Drury, Jill and Peter, *A Tisbury History* (Tisbury Books, 1980)

Dukes County Intelligencer, Vol. 31 No. 4, May 1990, and Vol. 32 No. 2, Nov. 1990

Eisenstedt. Martha's Vineyard (Oxmoor House, 1988)

Everyman Encyclopaedia (J.M. Dent)

Falkus, M. and Gillingham, J., *Historical Atlas of Britain* (Book Club Associates, 1981)

Garmonsway, G.N. (transl.), *Anglo-Saxon Chronicles* (Dent, Everyman's Library, 1953)

Goodall, John S., *The Story of an English Village* (Macmillan, 1978)

Harding, John, *Our Bells and the Life surrounding Them*

Harfield, A.B., *A History of the Village of Chilmark and Guide to the Parish Church* (1961)

Huntington, Gale, *Introduction to Martha's Vineyard* (Dukes County Historical Society, 1969)

Magnusson, Magnus (transl.), *The Vinland Sagas* (Penguin, 1965)

Melville, Herman, *Moby Dick* (Oxford University Press)

Morriss, B. (ed.), *Encyclopaedia of American History* (Harper and Row, Bicentennial edition)

New England Company, *A Short Note and History* [of the Society for the Propagation of the Gospel in New England]

Norton, Henry Franklin, *Martha's Vineyard. History and Legends* (Pyne Printing, 1923)

Pugh, R.B. (Ed.), *The Victoria History of the Counties of England. A History of Wiltshire, Vol. III* (University of London Institute of Historical Research)

Sinclair, Iona (Ed.), *The Pyramid and the Urn. The Life in Letters of a Restoration Squire* (Alan Sutton Publishing Ltd, 1994)

St Margaret's Church, Chilmark 1280–1980. 700th anniversary commemorative booklet.

Swanton, John R., *The Indian Tribes of North America* (Smithsonian Institution Press, City of Washington, 1974)

Syrett, David, *The Royal Navy in American Waters 1775–83* (Scolar Press)

Tanner, Heather and Robin, *A Wiltshire Village* (Impact Books, 1939)

Travers, Milton A., *The Wampanoag Indian Federation of the Algonquin Nation* (Christopher Publishing House, Boston, 1961)

Webb, Mary, *The Golden Arrow* (Virago, 1983)

Lightning Source UK Ltd.
Milton Keynes UK
UKHW03f1225100918
328641UK00005B/670/P

9 781906 978112